# Five-Legged Louie

Story by
**Christine Ann Gowey, and
Dr. Brandie Gowey, NMD**

Illustrations by
**Dr. Brandie Gowey, NMD**

Cover and Book Design by
**Charlotte Fox**

Edited by
**Charlotte Fox**

Copyright © 2018 Brandie Gowey, Christine Ann Gowey
Published by DR. DNA Press, Flagstaff, AZ

All Rights Reserved. No part of this book may be reproduced or distributed in any form or by any means without the prior written permission of the authors.

ISBN 978-1-947652-11-8
Printed in the United States of America

The Authors of this Work are not dispensing medical or life advice, or prescribing any treatment or technique, for any reason. This Work is merely intended to entertain and inspire thought-provoking discussions of life among adults and children alike. This Work is only intended to provide inspiration and information, and as such, the Authors of this Work assume no responsibility for your actions.

Proceeds from the sale of this book benefit medical research at the DR. DNA Clinic.
Learn more at *goweyresearchgroup.com*.

Louie's story is dedicated to everyone who has challenges in life.

He wants you to know that even if your life doesn't seem perfect, people care about you, help is available, and that with a positive attitude...

### Anything is Possible!

Louie was a handsome six-legged walking stick.

You could often find him sunning himself on Mrs. Dewdrop's mailbox, where she left books for him to read.

He always put on sunscreen before he settled in for some time in the sun with his latest novel.

One day, while Louie was enjoying the sun, Mrs. Dewdrop came out to the mailbox to say hello.

She put a letter in the mailbox and chatted with Louie about the lovely day.

After closing the door to the mailbox, she accidentally swiped the flag across Louie and damaged one of his legs!

Mrs. Dewdrop was very sorry for what happened. She cared about Louie! He was her friend!

Louie said, "Accidents do happen! Thank you for your concern and for the bandages, too! Normally, walking stick legs grow back, so I'm sure my leg will be fine."

The summer went on.
Louie continued to enjoy
his mailbox time.

He also spent time amongst
the leaves in the nearby
raspberry patch.

Mrs. Dewdrop noticed Louie's leg was not improving, so she offered to take him to see Doctor Ant.

Louie told Doctor Ant what had happened. "Mrs. Dewdrop and I are concerned because my leg is not growing back," Louie said.

Doctor Ant explained to Louie, "To properly heal, you have to have enough minerals, vitamins, water, and exercise.

"You also have to stay positive and rest between your exercise routines."

Louie  D.O.B. 1-04-15

# CHART

- [x] eat vegetables for minerals
- [ ] eat fruit for vitamins
- [ ] drink clean water for minerals and hydration
- [ ] exercise daily
- [ ] stay positive
- [ ] Rest

Signed _Doctor Ant_

Even though he was saddened over the loss of his leg, Louie decided he was going to give his best effort to becoming healthier.

He climbed trees.

He hopped from leaf to leaf in the raspberry patch.

He did crunches on the mailbox.

He even climbed the chimes to do his yoga routine.

Overall, Louie was beginning to feel very well.

One day while he was out for his morning workout, he heard a beautiful sound. He went to see what it was.

It was his friend Tymbal, and the Tymbal Bob Orchestra!

The music filled the air!

Louie listened closely,
and as he listened,
he began to dance.

As he danced, his five legs
rubbed together. And as his
five legs rubbed together,
they made music!

And Oh! What wonderful
music his five legs made!

The music was so lovely that Tymbal stopped his orchestra so he could listen.

"Louie," he said, "you are making the most wonderful music! Might you be able to join my orchestra?"

Louie thought about it and asked, "Is it a problem that I only have five legs?"

"A problem?" Tymbal exclaimed. "No! If you had six legs," he told him, "the music might not be as delightful!"

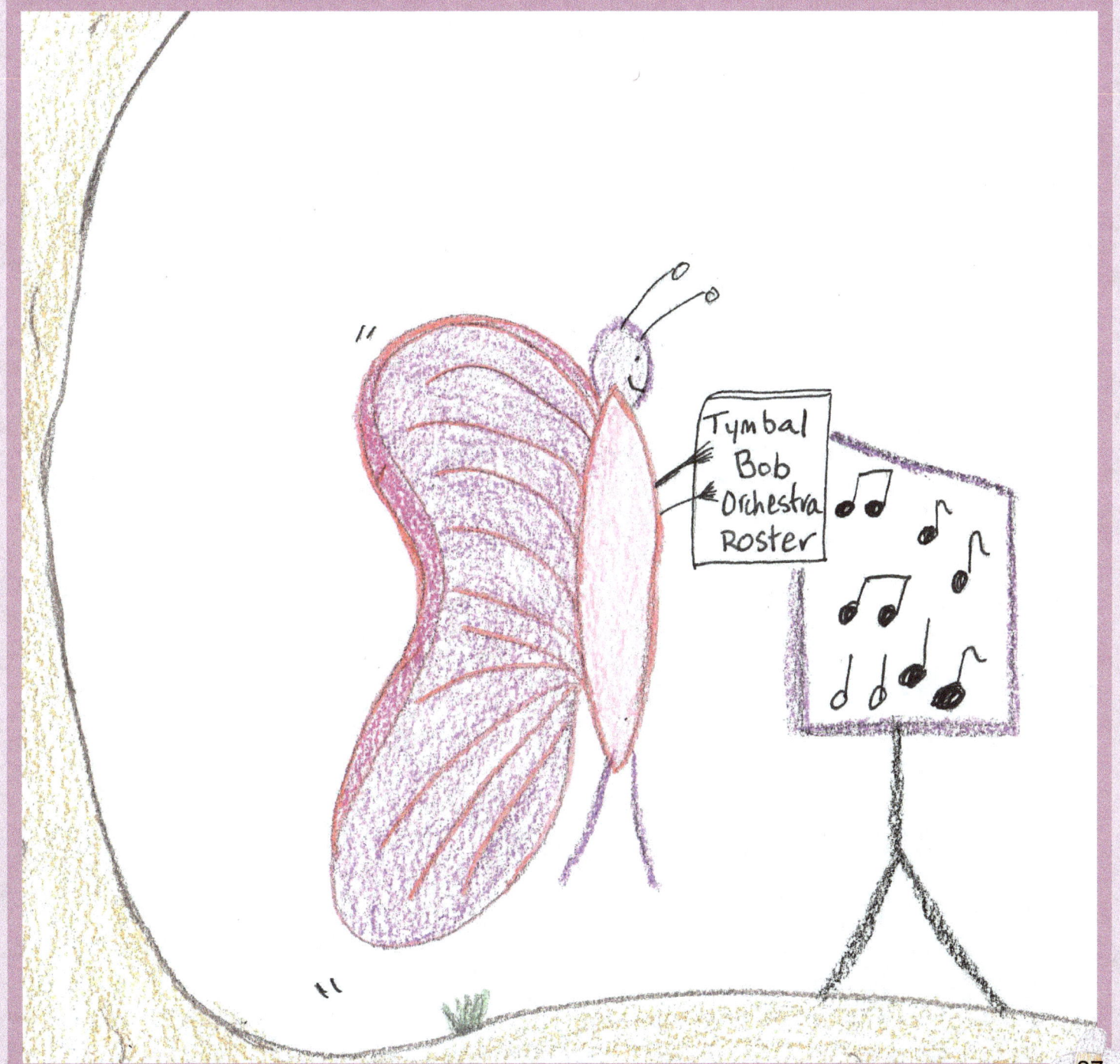

And so it was that Louie joined the Tymbal Bob Orchestra. He added a key of music that had been missing!

From that day on, Louie never thought of having only five legs as a problem.

He thought of it as having a Possibility!

# From the Desk of Louie

Never think that you can't do something!

Every challenge in life is only a possibility and opportunity to become a better person or artist.

You never know what you can do if you keep yourself strong and healthy!

## Anything is Possible!

Love,
Louie

www.ingramcontent.com/pod-product-compliance
Lightning Source LLC
Chambersburg PA
CBHW081340080526
44588CB00017B/2693